Help

by Kirsten Minschke
Illustrated by Norm Perez

M000073711

HOSPITAL

PEARSON

Glenview, Illinois • Boston, Massachusetts • Chandler, Arizona
Upper Saddle River, New Jersey

Mom heard her son crying.
"Alan! What's wrong?" asked Mom.
"Help! I fell off my bike."

Mom called 9-1-1 on her phone.
"My son fell off his bike!" said Mom.
"Please come now!"

Max and Emma came to help.
"What is wrong?" asked Max.

"I hurt my leg," said Alan.
Emma helped Alan.
Emma looked at Alan's leg.

"Let's go to the hospital," said Emma.
"We need to take an X-ray of your leg," said Max.

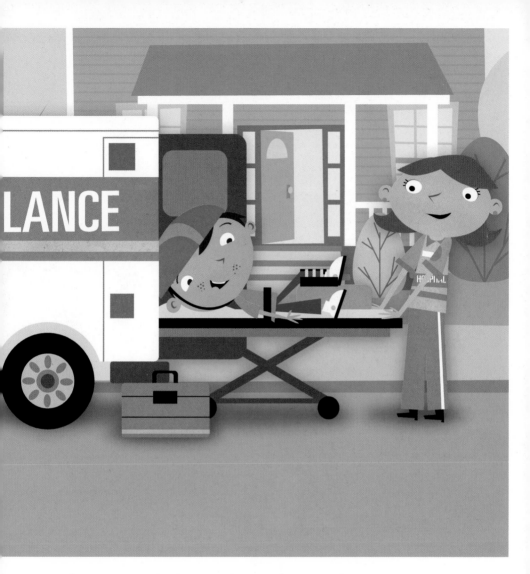

"I hope I did not break my leg," said Alan.
"The X-ray will show us," said Emma.

cast

Alan's leg was broken.
Emma put a cast on Alan's leg.
"How do you feel?" asked Emma.
"I feel better!" said Alan.